LOVE'S LABORS

LOVE'S LABORS

BRENT NEWSOM

CavanKerry ◈ Press LTD.

CavanKerry Press Ltd.
Fort Lee, New Jersey
www.cavankerrypress.org

Publisher's Cataloging-in-Publication
(Provided by Quality Books, Inc.)

Newsom, Brent.
[Poems. Selections]
Love's labors / Brent Newsom. -- First edition.
pages cm
Poems.
ISBN 978-1-933880-52-5

I. Title.

PS3614.E723A6 2015   811'.6
QBI14-600187

Cover photograph by Corey Lee Fuller
Cover and interior text design by Gregory Smith
First Edition 2015, Printed in the United States of America

CavanKerry Press is dedicated to springboarding the careers of previously unpublished, early, and mid-career poets by bringing to print two to three Emerging Voices annually. Manuscripts are selected from open submission; Cavankerry Press does not conduct competitions.

CavanKerry Press is grateful for the support it receives from the New Jersey State Council on the Arts.

This project is supported in part by an award from the National Endowment for the Arts. To find out more about how NEA grants impact individuals and communities, visit www.arts.gov.

For my family

CONTENTS

III

IV

V

FOREWORD

At one point in *Love's Labors,* Brent Newsom addresses his child, thirty weeks in utero: "If I have wisdom," he writes,

> it's this: question miracles
> and believe,
> for you are one
> and you aren't.

Miracles will always be questionable, of course, yet we can't help but believe in the author's wisdom, finding in his work a scope and resourcefulness that do feel miraculous, even as they feel non-miraculous, in the sense that Newsom pays the keenest and ultimately the most loving attention to the quotidian lives of his collection's creatures.

Love's Labors is punctuated by those addresses to his and his wife's forthcoming son, and the poems allow us almost personally to participate in all the joy, awe, fear, irritation, and love that such expectation inevitably engenders, with an emphasis, at last, on the joy and love. That love, however, extends in countless other directions.

Newsom applies it to local characters like his G.I. grunt, Pfc. Mason Buxton, who harbors impulses as violent as his Iraqi deployment requires, even as his deep humanity—however he may wish to mask it—shines through. We both weep and smile as well when the widow Esther Green, availing herself of her late husband's insurance, moves from a trailer park to her first dwelling with an actual lawn, a move that might signal release—were it not for Esther's feeling the abiding ache of the dead man's absence, and of the simple pleasures they shared in their time together. Throughout the collection, too, we encounter the roguish Floyd Fontenot, a figure whom a less perceptive and compassionate observer than Newsom would heedlessly dismiss as a mere redneck. Floyd *is* a redneck, but, characteristically, Newsom moves beyond such a bigoted impression to find the human heart that beats within Floyd, as within us all. Newsom's regard for such men and women, at last, closely illustrates the Greek notion of *agape*.

There is many another character as well, so skillfully limned that by book's end we feel we know each as thoroughly as we might had they appeared in a long novel—or, more accurately, shown up as our own neighbors. To afford portraiture so compelling within the confines of poetry is one of the signal accomplishments of *Love's Labors*. But Newsom can manage such an effect even within the constraints of a sonnet like "How Floyd Fontenot Lost His Father." That he can do so—well, the word *miracle* rushes back to mind.

Let me linger on the narrative of that very sonnet to extend the theme of my commentary here. A précis of its story would run like this: Floyd's father has a heart attack as he masturbates, watching a pornographic movie stolen from his own son.

Imagine that you heard *only* that précis. I suspect that, like me, you'd be inclined to turn away in disgust. But read the sonnet closely when you come to it; your sympathy and affection for both Floyd and his father—however grudgingly accorded—will, again, strike you as miraculous.

But the secret of Newsom's success in *Love's Labors* will be no secret at all by collection's end. The triumph of his poems, one and all, lies in the author's intimate and personal knowledge of the characters he presents, from his soldier in the killing field, to the lovely local bartender Patti, to the beloved woman who will parent the coming son with him, to a doubt-haunted local preacher's wife.

Very shortly ago, my own local preacher left a note to be read at his funeral. It included a warning: *Beware! Non-judgment day is coming!* This brilliant series of poems conveys a similar message. The vigor and resourcefulness of Brent Newsom's language and his varied formats—from the most strictly conventional to the most wide-open free verse—would be enough to command our applause; marry these to the wisdom I mentioned at the outset, and to a fellow-feeling that far transcends mere toleration, and you have, as you will soon see, a work not only artful but also, if we attend to its example, morally improving.

One can't ask much more of poetry.

—*Sydney Lea*

And to the angel of the church in Smyrna write: . . . I know your tribulation and your poverty (but you are rich).

—Revelation 2:8-9

LOVE'S
LABORS

I

Smyrna

By a strip of highway spilled beside a swamp
that exhales sphinx moths and hums mosquito hymns:
their kids sack out on sofas while the men
make sweatless love to tired wives, then go
perspire in oil-smeared, orange hard hats
on caffeinated graveyard shifts. Days off,
they jaw across their truck beds lined with cans
in the gravel lot outside the donut shop.
Come winter, dawn and dusk, they tramp the bogs
with shotguns, taking life as it comes to them.
Pass through and you'll be met with friendly waves
and icy stares. At the edge of town, by the caution light,
a metal sign, green, lettered in white:
WELCOME—riddled with steel shot.

Esther Green Plans a Funeral

Lord knows, Claudia, I can't have it
at the church. Bill quit years ago,
once the girls were grown,
said it wasn't worth the trouble
of putting on slacks and his good white shirt
to be patronized by neckties and comb-overs.

He'd still have himself a Sabbath
of sorts—I'd come home to him sitting outside
in his faded flannel and jeans,
handsome even leaned back in a lawn chair
smoking his Winstons.
He'd ask how the sermon was,
follow me in to help with lunch.

It was one of those Sunday lunches
when I noticed red flecks
on the whisker-tips of his mustache.
He'd choked it back who knows how long.
Don't mince words, he told the doc,
so she said the spot was softball-sized,
the rest of his lung likely black
as a burnt marshmallow.
She showed us a malignant cell—
looked like those prickly sweetgum balls
that fall to the ground in winter.
Only softer, a pill of lint almost.
Next day, Bill went back to work,
which was not a big surprise.
He lasted weeks, which was.

Ode to the Heart

sixteen weeks

1

Beyond lithe triceps, bulging biceps,
above taut calves and washboard abs,
unsurpassed by lats and hams
is our mother muscle hustling
blood through her brood of tubes,
muscle by which all other muscles flex.

2

What-what-what-what-what-
wafts through the Doppler mic
held against the slight, gelled
swell of your mother's uterus.
Your body's first voice
utters a stutter
I have no answer for.

3

Praise the four-chambered
orchestra playing staccato
sonate da camera in your chest,
percussive as the timpani,
or more so: *allegro, vivace, presto*—
how would Mozart mark
one hundred sixty sixteenth notes
per sixty seconds? *Prestissimo.*

4

We'll take you home to four small rooms,
one just for you: your name brilliant
in bubbled letters, glass balloons
like buoys in the corner. Your mother
pressing you to her breast, we'll step
into our asthmatic old apartment,
an April wind rushing in behind,
fresh oxygen borne in our blood.

Pfc. Mason Buxton Wets a Hook

All warfare is based on deception.
                    —Sun Tzu, *The Art of War*

Whether you're wiping out a phantom weapons cache
or planting homemade bombs in cardboard boxes,
trash cans, saddlebags—Sun Tzu was right:
the lie lies dead at the heart of war. By it
we live and die. The art's in choosing lures.
(A shiner? Melon lizard? Chartreuse worm?)
That's part. But a naked lie won't nail a bass.
You hide the hook inside. Then drop the bait
between two cypress stumps, jig your rod
at five Mississip, crack open a cold one. Sip.
He bites, you set and reel—then watch the lake explode.

An American Love Affair

The whole idea of riding atop a series of contained explosions was abhorrent to many.
> —Edwin Black, *Internal Combustion*

In fact, it seemed a marriage made in hell.
To ride astride ignited gas and spot
a hefty dowry for the right—why not
store a load of TNT in the tire well?
It was courting disaster, seemed vaguely like sin,
so thousands jilted the car. Was it some joke,
this notion of motion? They smelled the noxious smoke
that drifted from beneath its flawless skin.

But that exhaust became a tart's *parfum:*
enter Henry Ford, his Model T
a winsome mistress masses could afford,
a locomotive whore. America swooned—
enamored, moved, driven to ecstasy.
We paved. We drilled, refined. We spilled. We warred.

Internal Combustion

Combustion is not an explosion.
> —John L. Lumley, *Engines: An Introduction*

Not, as I'd pictured, the aftermath of bombs
erupting (no severed limbs, no scattered shrapnel,
no razed villages, no cratered fields of battle,
no racing, roiling, fiery balls of napalm
like you see in grainy films from Vietnam,
no mushroom cloud arising from the rubble)
inside a wrist-sized, lathed aluminum capsule
where pumping pistons POW! and BOOM! and KA-BLAM!

It's more the measured pulse of AK-fire
and M-16s discharging ammunition
in Basra's dusty streets, Tikrit, Ad-Dawr;
the careful missiles riding laser wires
to Baghdad's hidden armories. Combustion
is tidy violence: a spark fed fuel and air.

Pfc. Mason Buxton Embraces the Suck

Back home in the Louisiana night, my wife
squeezes the hand of some ponytailed nurse,
cursing my name with every push
while I wake again in the cradle
of fucking civilization, another day
the same, decked out in battle rattle,
lugging an idiot stick, extra mags
stuffed in my flak jacket, roam
the same brown streets and wait
for necktied Beltway clerks
to sort out this Sunni and Shiite shit—
and I can almost hear her grunts and groans
and the crunch of ice between her teeth,
almost see her lips wrenching with pain
as the doctor inserts the forceps into her
and tells her, *Again,* and, *One more,* and she screams—
and from a hundred feet I feel the blast
behind me and tuck beneath the rain
of dirt and rock, then sidle along a wall
and turkey peek around the corner,
see vics spread-eagled on the ground,
some dead, some dying eyes-wide-open
in the arms of women already wearing black,
and at the checkpoint, a pool of blood
and fur, a donkey ear (*Shock and
hee-haw,* we call it later), then I'm holding
a soldier whose arm hangs from his shoulder
by shreds of sinew and skin.
A month goes by, and I'm at Ft. Living Room.
I have a daughter and lie awake in bed,
sleepless at oh three hundred,
seeing behind my eyes the placid sun
hung like a medal in the bone-colored sky.

Agriculture

twenty-one weeks

The three-finger salute, the sonographer says,
as though you're giving me the bird
discreetly: your two femurs
brackets around your penis—
an underside view of you
transcribed from sound to image.
A boy. For a moment I feel
some mystical male bond already
shooting roots into the earth.

But someday you will hate me
as I hated my cash-strapped father
when he planted five acres of peas to sell
the summer I turned thirteen,
woke me each day before dawn
to pace the rows with a bushel basket.
One afternoon, customers watching,
I told him I quit. Red-faced and sweating,
he rose to his six-feet-one, roared, *Boy,*
you're not going anywhere. So I wasn't.

Now, from this doctor's office dimmed
to just your greenish onscreen glow,
I see my dad was a good one and loved
persistently, if too quietly,
perplexed at times by my zeal
and my silences. Boy, your hate
will be our harvest, the grain we glean
from the seed of some failing
I cannot yet name. May we gather it into sheaves
and grind it into flour. Let us bake whole
loaves, son, of bread we both can eat.

Esther Green Moves Out of the Sunset Acres Mobile Home Community

1

Every day, more faded ghosts
of family past: last week,
cleaning out a drawer, photos
I didn't know you'd kept. Me and you
holding cane poles with bluegill on the lines,
you beaming while I squint
into the sun; Easter, me and our girls
dolled up in white straw hats,
matching floral dresses I sewed
from *McCall's* patterns; our youngest
graduating elementary the year before
she drowned. And one of me
before kids, *The Queen*
inked on back in blue.

2

Weekends, England's queen camps out
in Windsor Castle, the Union Jack
flying high to show she's home.
On the pristine lawn, she lets loose
whichever four corgis she's brought along.
All this I learned from the satellite's
Biography channel, which you would never watch
with me. *People's private lives,*
you'd say and rise, heading outside
for a smoke. But what's private
about being queen? If you were here
you'd listen to what I liked the best:
a whole room in the state apartments
covered with portraits. Alive with spirits.

3

No one's left inside the wood-grain walls
of our double-wide kingdom:
the girls both off making their own babies
with common-law husbands-to-be,
then bringing the dears for yearly visits;
you gone. But even without our furniture's
sagging fleurs-de-lis, I could read
our history there—a dull brown crest
in the carpet where our oldest bled
after busting her scalp on the table's edge,
the lines in the avocado vinyl where,
for each night's supper, you scooted in.

4

Raise a flag. Make it black, half-mast.
Your insurance bought this two-bedroom:
brand new oven, my first lawn, an old pecan.
But a scratch in the hardwood floor
is just a scratch. The walls all stare
at me blankly as strangers, so I tape up
a photo—the one with the bluegill—
then set to unpacking, you
beaming down at all the boxes.

Saint Gerard

thirty-eight weeks

I help her on with the gown, a cotton curtain,
paisley print fringed with ties and metal snaps
but no arm holes or back, nothing we feel safe
calling a neckline. Her lips move as if in prayer.
I wrap the gown around her, press the rivets home,
then bow the ties behind. This looks like love.

A sudden cramping after we made love.
Her labor starting? No. Now she's certain.
It's not her time. She wants to go back home.
I drove us here. She starts to cry and I snap
at her: *It's too late to leave.* On the wall, a prayer
to Saint Gerard, patron of the pregnant, for safe

delivery. I mumble maxims: *better safe*
and so on. My fear for the child has trumped my love
for her. Lying down, she trembles like cornered prey.
Though we're alone, we draw the striped curtain.
A nurse enters. A latex glove snaps
against a wrist, and two lubed fingers home

in on her cervix, press toward the child's home
these past nine months. She grimaces. I'm safe,
seated beside the bed. I watch, and she snaps
her head away, to hide the face I love.
Something's descended, a heavy, opaque curtain
of silence hanging between us. I read the prayer

on the wall and recall, she asked me to pray
an hour ago, while we were still at home.
I said I would. Then a magician's curtain
closed, and *poof!*—just smoke and lights. A heist; a safe
emptied of compassion. An inside job. What's love
if not the patience to pray? Guilt's whip snaps

at my back. *Mea culpa.* How I wish I could snap
my fingers, be back on our saggy couch, and pray:
God of peace, make mine a patient love,
and free from fear. She turns. Her eyes plead, *Home.*
The nurse agrees. Mother and child are sound, safe.
I exhale, then help her dress, draw back the curtain.

At home, my penance of final touches: the nursery's curtains,
safety plugs, old frames prepared for new snapshots.
And this: to pray that I might learn, and relearn, love.

II

Epithalamion

for Amanda

Welcome to where we dwell
in the wounds that we inflict

on one another—another
way of saying, on ourselves.

Injured, we limp and drift
through dim-lit corridors,

sift cupboards for salves
the other has stashed

away. Here the paneled walls
close in, all tongues

and grooves, scab over
like mending skin.

Two (another
another) too

many here,
and none

too few,
we join,

grafted: scion
and stock,

your skin on
my burn.

Mathematics

Between white sheets we solve for x.
We add, subtract, again and again,
our figures cleaving and being cleft.
The body's mystery arithmetic:
one plus one is one.

But tonight our parts add up to more than their sum,
the calculus now yields a new derivative.
No formula for this, no theorem. Unsolvable equation:
some hidden, unknown term, some independent variable, remains.
1 cell begins its long division—2, then 4, then 8—our multiplication.

Floyd and Patti

The JC Cocktail Palace: a dive
with self-delusions. But it was theirs,
the place where Floyd tipped biggest
and Patti kept 'em coming.
When he asked if he could be the piston
pumping in her cylinder,
she had the wit to say,
I'm not a four-stroke
kind of woman, and the good sense
to slap him.
He was smitten.

He was persistent. She liked
the attention, came to crave
his viscous gaze dripping

       from face
       to tits
       to ass
       to thigh
       to calf.

In his Charger parked beneath the pink
glow of the Palace's neon sign,
one night, after closing, she caved.
Still kissing, they clambered
over the console, unzipped,
and the crankshaft of his hips
spun in the sump of hers.
Somehow, though, he missed

what she gauged even then:
that they wouldn't make it far
with so little in the tank.
Not even on a fire like theirs.
Not even with a white-hot spark.

Desire

It arrives on your doorstep
swaddled like an orphan.
You glance around, check
the mailbox for a note. Nothing.
You feed it. It grows, begins
to walk, helps itself
to the olives in the fridge,
sucking out the pimentos
and spitting them on the counter.
Before long, it's lounging
in its underwear, scratching itself,
telling you, *I'm hungry,*
make me a sandwich.
Tuna, no crust.

Or you starve it,
shut it in a coat closet
for weeks under a heap
of forgotten shoes, turn the TV up
till its crying stops and you kill
the noise, soak in the silence,
believe things are back
the way they were.
But when everything's still
and you lie awake in bed,
it whooshes about the house
singing your name
in the thin, bright tones
of a castrato.

Floyd Fontenot's Friday Night

Cars are easier than people,
he thinks. You can find the failing part
and fix it, just replace what doesn't work—
worn clutch, busted fuel pump—
and you'll be on your way again.
Cause, effect.
Things are fine
as long as he can work,
which is why he's in the garage, bent
beneath the hood of a Crown Vic
at eight o'clock on a Friday night,
cleaning spark plugs and gaskets,
feeling for cracks
in the belts and hoses.

He knows Patti hated
how he'd take apart her problems,
listen like she was an engine
full of knocks and pings,
a thing to disassemble and diagnose,
a thing he could repair
given the right tools. Fixing things
was all he knew to do. She'd cry.
His patience would break down
just like old motor oil
and leave the kind of friction
that leads to lasting damage.
The night before she cruised
right out of Smyrna, Floyd flipped
the kitchen table, supper plates and all.

Later, maybe, after the Owls game
will have ended in defeat, he'll head over
to Mason Buxton's or Buster Henry's,
talk up a game of cards. Or maybe settle
in his kitchen with the tall square bottle
he'd raced his Charger
to the parish line to buy. But first
he'll drive the sheriff's squad car
down past the donut shop
and around the block,
to listen to it purr.

At the Clinic

five weeks

Peanut-shaped, in the nurse's words.
I picture the appetizers
that come before the appetizers
at my hometown's only steakhouse,
how we flick the brittle husks
to the hardwood planks beneath our feet,
pop the nuts in our mouths
between lemony sips of tea.

Leaving the sterile exam room's glare,
we munch on the bite-sized facts
fed us with practiced zest
by a heavyset nurse with tattooed wrists:
already you have a spinal cord,
arms and legs beginning to bud,
a heart that started gently pulsing
ten days back. Already you are male
or female.

       For weeks to come, stories
of stillbirth or miscarriage—futile
distinction we'll learn nonetheless—
will flock in on the wind, an unkindness
of black-winged birds drawn to feed
on every seed of hope or dream
that drops to the ground. Hard-eyed
and hook-beaked, they'll perch heavily
on a line, settle in while we pretend
not to hear their ravenous caws.

Acorns crunch underfoot in the parking lot.
The first crisp break from arid heat, a charge
in the early autumn air. I voice a pledge
to always love, protect, allow no hungry claw
to harm you. Listen. Are the two
proto-lobes of your brain
celled enough for you to hear
my shaky tenor, muffled
by the wall of your mother's body?
Inch-long offspring—peanut-shaped thing—
do you catch the crack in my voice?
Promises no man could keep,
no god would deign to make.

Ash Wednesday

Now that the penitents down the road
at Our Lady of Prompt Succor
are done with the beads and doubloons,
the parties, parades, and ring-shaped king cakes,
Claudia Blackwood is happy for Smyrna's return
to a rhythm of industry, ready
as ever for New Hope to begin
rehearsing again
for the annual Easter pageant.
Tonight after practice they'll all get fitted,
find out what needs to be altered,
so all day she launders costumes,
purges the odor of mothballs
from old polyester and cotton.
She tugs out a tangle of robes from the dryer,
drops them into a plastic basket.
Around her head she drapes a shawl
and inhales the clean perfume—spring fresh
—of dryer sheets. She repeats her line,
straining for Magdalene's breathless glee:

> *I have seen the Lord!*
> *I have seen the Lord!*
> *I have seen the Lord!*

Fête

eight weeks

Embryon, to Homer: *young animal.*
To later Greeks: *fruit.*
Metaphors mixing like drinks
amid the riddle
of your unformed body
accruing form as a word
accrues meaning: crude
creature-seed budding
deep in the furrow
of your mother's body.
She's curled in bed already
when I propose a toast.
Today, the doctors say,
you graduate to *fetus*—a word
borne to the English tongue
by Latin and, buried
deeper down, a root
connoting *to come into being.*
So: come on, come in. Be well.
In seven months we'll greet you
in your native parlance:
baby, from *babe,* from *baban,*
from an infant's bubbly
first attempts at utterance.
Hence this quiet fête, our son,
or daughter: to you we raise
a crystal glass. Of water.

III

Terror

They know they all will die eventually:
the swordsman barking his razor-edged

outrageous ultimatums gets sniped but swipes
his oaken blade across the neck of a hostage

begging mercy. IEDs erupt. In slow-mo, boys collapse,
loft grenades, empty clips, spit fully automatic

rifle sounds from their trilling tongues until
they all lie still, suck in lungfuls of air

sticky with sap and bubblegum. Every day for a week
Pfc. Mason Buxton has idled at the four-way

on his slow drive home from work. Today it's war
again in the junky corner lot, a battlefield ideal

(barricades of corrugated tin, cypress knees as mines,
pine cone grenades, empty beer can car bomb

planted in the abandoned, rust-encrusted Pontiac)
for dirt-filmed schoolboys to split themselves

into terrorists and troops. Windows down,
he hears them yelling where they fell

as his dented pickup's *Semper Fi* front plate
finally drifts by. They count their wounds: soft hands

with pine cone pockmarks, bull's-eye bruises on skinny backs,
suntanned neck rubbed blood red, old scabs scraped fresh—

how they'll burn in the bath tonight.

Strawberries

ten weeks

You cannot come soon enough
for your mother, vomiting
strawberries in the bathroom, the strawberries
I bought for her because they are rich
in folic acid, and folic acid is good,
the nurse says, for your brain;
so I bought them for your brain,
put the plastic carton in the cart myself
since I now shop for groceries
so your mother can rest and eat
crackers every so often,
something to settle her stomach
so she will not throw up the folic acid
—but there, suspended in toilet water,
half-digested strawberries
looking like some awful afterbirth,
and your mother spits,
then rinses her mouth,
trudges back to our bed
pledging to be done with strawberries,
and I am caught between
please be normal
and *we will love you if you aren't*
as I hold down the lever, watch
the deep red swirl of bile and berries.

Horticulture

Mid-June, a gangly, wide-eyed eight-year-old
with pinkish, peach-fuzzed Dumbo ears
oversoaped the dishes his first night,
deliberately, gleeful as soapsuds spewed
from the Kenmore onto the kitchen tiles.
I went for the mop while, firm but calm,
the Director sent the boy to bed, which he also wet
deliberately.
              I didn't go home that college summer
but part-timed as a nursery vendor
at a big-box lawn and garden center—
made "color" the first thing "guests" would see,
trimmed leaves gone brown with drought or disease—
and interned at the ranch for troubled boys,
hired-hand-slash-babysitter (*Role model,*
the Director said. *A presence*)
with a furnished, private room, rent-free.
Discipline was not in the intern's job description,
so Dumbo clipped my heels, yakking with candor
while I pulled squash and young cucumber
or set an iron fencepost, pretended to listen,
which should have been enough. A presence.

He felt so deeply I felt embarrassed
when he spoke of why his mother left him
with grandparents (now I can't recall—
the psych ward, drug habit, jail?)
and of why his grandma and grandpa left him
with us. *It made me hurt inside,*
he said, *but I know they're too old
to keep a kid.* He was wiser in that way,
and more mature, than I, unacquainted
with such frankness and such grief.

But on the ranch's hard red dirt, tenderness
was taboo. Ten feet up the climbing wall,
he screamed. The others jeered as he clung
too stiffly, then slipped. He wailed,
knowing only the rope I held
saved him from falling. He'd felt those lines
go slack before. His dusty sneakers strained
for solid ground, and when they touched
he clung to my waist, rivulets on his dirty cheeks,
snot quivering on his upper lip. He needed
more than I knew how to give.

I volunteered for extra hours at work,
preferred to pluck dead blades from sprays
of purple fountain grass, arrange displays
of garish zinnias, set pallets of young crepe myrtles
outside the gate. I lined up pots of hostas
straight as rails in a white pipe fence,
napped on patio chairs whenever I could.
Evenings, I unrolled a rubber hose,
gave everything another splash of water.
The caladiums leaned toward me, giant
green-veined ears eavesdropping on my prayers
for autumn.   By August he was gone;
but I still felt the weight of him, hanging
in mid-air by the rope that linked our bodies
like an umbilical cord, still heard his voice
grow shrill and dry before I let him down.

New Hope Baptist Church

Where the Savior's left foot ought to be,
a jagged absence. A yawning hole in the glass
patched with opaque, dull gray tape
for years, ever since the summer night
a thunderstorm flung in a branch.
The western sun once washed right through that foot's
gold skin, like the knees bent under their burden
and the torso slivered with crimson shards,
which shoulders a brown crossbeam.
On the opposite wall at sunset ever since,
the watery image of a gold-toned Christ
lugs a shadow behind him, dragging
a dark club foot along his via dolorosa.

Now Pastor wants it repaired
by Easter. Says, *The Lord's house,*
the Lord's house. Says, *We*
have printed special yellow envelopes,
says, *The plate will be passed.*
At the early evening business meeting,
Esther Green stands, smooths her dress,
says, *What about the impoverished?*
The sick, the addicted, the lame,
the lonely? Says, *What*
about doing unto the least of these?
Pastor cues the pianist, says, *The poor*
will always be with you. Says, *The Lord's house,*
the Lord's house. Says, *Come,*
let us pray.

First Ultrasound

thirteen weeks

Six feet tall in your diaper and sky blue onesie,
you unlatch and tell your mom to fetch some meat:
Woman, never mind that I have no teeth—
your breasts are dry, and I'm still bloody hungry.

She recounts the dream for me while we eat breakfast.
"So. Nursing's the thing," I ask, "you fear the most?"
A pause. "One of them," she sobs into her toast.
Hormones, morning. A stupid question. Reckless.

Later, awaiting your first ultrasound,
a sudden second answer comes: you're not
inside—there's nothing there, the test was botched.
Filming's begun, but the lead cannot be found.

Then your screen debut: head, torso, webby hands—
a preening little star with big demands.

Inheritance

Flat as a man on his deathbed, I lie on the ground.
I'm twenty-six. Ten years too late to start
tinkering like this, but I never cared
about cars—a subject that seemed miles removed
from basketball or books—back when I'd hand
a wrench to that shade-tree grease monkey, my father,

and then go back to shooting hoops. Now my father
rattles orders down through the ancient engine, ground
against which I search, with flashlight and groping hand,
for the black figure of a cylinder. There. The starter.
Three-eighths socket, he says, *two mounting bolts to remove.*
It's my granddad's truck, now passed into my care.

I could sell it for a couple hundred bucks, but I care
too much, for now. The filthy cab still holds my granddad's
smell—cut grass and spilled gas. The key, never removed.
No need. With so much dirt and oil ground
into the seat, no thief would bother. From the start
it was a beast of burden, bought third-hand

for hauling his machines. Like disembodied hands
on the dash, the gloves I always spurned, too "tough" to care
about blisters, even when I was too small to start
the mowers myself. In the eyes of my granddad
a fresh-mown lawn, properly edged, was sacred ground—
wildness tamed, sin wiped clean, a stain removed.

Autumn now. No yards to mow. Six months removed
from his last breath, and the truck has been handed
down to me, who spent hot summers pacing the ground
behind his loud Lawn-Boys. I learned that faithful care
for what's not yours, and pride in your labor (like a father's
in his son), and light enough to finish what you start

are each a kind of grace. I pull off the starter.
Seems simple enough—replace what's been removed,
revive what's died. I crawl free, discover my dad
bent over me, reaching for my greasy hand.
I examine the truck: a patient under doctor's care,
surgical instruments scattered on the ground.

It still won't start. It needs rebuilding from the ground
up. Intensive care. We give in, as if removing
a respirator. I follow my dad inside to wash my hands.

How Floyd Fontenot Lost His Father

at the cardiologist's office

Without a single ping or knock of warning
the sputtering engine of his father's heart
stalled, and though they tried for half the morning,
the doctors couldn't get it to restart.

So goes the story Floyd will always tell.
His heart gave out all right, but with his dick
wrapped in his hand. He revved it up until
his ticker stopped, ogling a titty flick.

He'd stolen it from Floyd's own VCR
and left him with a forty dollar fine—
a rental lost. The clerk at SuperXXXstar
just winked: *No biggie, happens all the time.*

Now Floyd lies down, tries to keep his calm.
The paper beneath him crinkles when he shifts
his weight. The lights above him flicker and hum
just like the shop's. Except now *he's* on the lift,

shirtless, with the hair shaved from his chest.
The sterile, clinical air hangs dry and cold,
then electrodes read his father's one bequest—
unsettled accounts: what borrowed, bought, stolen, sold.

Turbulence

Air tumbles through the intake valve,
                              bends the flame front,
      folds, bends,
                 fills the chamber,
                                    thickens
that plane of fire once thin as the smooth page
                 on which you type
                              this turbulence of signs,
      whirl
                   of serifs and stems
        stamped on a leaf,
runes producing, or suggesting,
                            sound and sense.

Years ago a valve released in you,
                        sucked in a rush of wind
          you were certain would extinguish
                           the thin membrane of flame
              you found your faith was
                   while sitting beside a friend
on a rock
            by the Mimbres River,
                where nothing—not the stars
        that winked
            their ancient creation, not
the Mimbres   mumbling praise, not even
                         the cold
        that forced its way
                    into your bones
                   like sins of the flesh—
made sense anymore.

What air blew
  through you that night,
         turbulent,
     crumpled your belief
into a ball, like a draft
   destined for the wastebasket?
     That swirl of doubt
        distorted, true,
but all the while expanded
         that zone
   in which a flame might burn
   in you.

Floyd Fontenot, Free Bird

Better to die from his own
machination—to grease
himself, ha!—Floyd thinks beneath the Charger
he named Pearl, she painted creamy white
with two black racing stripes,
she of ceramic-coated headers
and hoses of stainless steel,
of chrome twenties and dual exhaust,
she of the blower through the hood.
Now she of the axles freshly lubed.

Fuck yes. Better that than break down
like a rusted-out beater
due to a shitty heart, birthright
of a Fontenot. Floyd knows the scum
sludging his own lines. His engine
was made for speed, not mileage,
and Fontenots run 'em hard and fast,
something Patti learned real quick.
The note she pinned against the windshield
beneath a wiper blade said, *Floyd,*
it sure as hell was a wild ride,
and she became one more name
on a long list of leavers.
But Floyd knows he has himself to blame
and too much of his old man in him.
He could never get at the source of the rattle,
hidden beneath a hood that won't release.

All he'd have to do is close the garage
with Pearl inside and fire her up,
maybe set the tuner to classic rock,
call in and request a Skynyrd song.
Then crank the volume up and the windows down.
Or maybe better, kick back and listen shut-eyed
to the metallic canter of the idling Hemi,
breathe in deep that dust cloud of exhaust.

IV

Christmas Day

twenty-six weeks

In bed this morning, I finally felt the kick
your mother's described for weeks to my dumb smile.
With your aunt expecting, too, we constitute
unwitting, incomplete nativities
around the den: two Marys in recliners,
your uncle and I two Josephs awaiting the blessed
events. A friend who knew such things once said
the stable was likely a cave, a room hewn out
of desert rock—not unlike a tomb.

Ritual requires we pose for a photograph,
document our growth—family of nine
this year, eleven next—so we file outside
where cardinals preen in the birdbath. We stand in rows
and smile into the merry winter light.
But the shot that we all ooh and aah about
shows two expectant mothers back to back.

This is as close to your cousin as you will come.
Ava will be cremated before you are born,
leaving your aunt and uncle only a box
of ashes they don't know where to spread.
Soon your aunt will spend sleepless nights
willing herself to feel the slightest stir.
For three long months my hand will gravitate
to the hollow cave beneath your mother's sweater.
But now the day plods on with typical cheer:
the electric noise of the boys with their R.C. cars,
their video games. The adults grazing on sweets
between hands of gin. Even the cardinals festive,
flashing their scarlet feathers at the feeder.

Ava

*All the days ordained for me
were written in your book
before one of them came to be.*
                    —Psalm 139:16

With pitocin the labor ends
in under two hours. No cry
pierces the morning air.
Next day, her parents drift
between nameless markers,
black granite obelisks, and angels
frozen in stone. The light
catches their inscrutable faces
in the smooth surface of marble
blank as the flyleaf of a book.

Needing a Day Away from Smyrna, Floyd Fontenot Winds Up in Baton Rouge, on the East Bank of the Mississippi

From the levee he'd heard the low-pitched roar
    beneath the calls of birds, a placid drone
        like the box fan Patti had always run
to help her sleep. His father had brought him here
    one Independence Day. They watched the fireworks
        burst over the bridge while his father swigged
from a pewter flask, some woman sitting on his lap.
    Floyd unlaces his boots. He wades in up to his knees,
        his waist. Leans in to the chilly current. It presses
against his right side, swirls in front and behind,
    closes back around his left. *I am a scab*
        in the river's skin, he thinks. He pitches forward,
goes under, and kicks, kicks hard and pulls
    against the water, his shirt sticking to his chest,
        keeps pulling and kicking, kicks across the current,
kicks against Patti who's left him and against
    his dead perverted father and the shoddy heart
        he gave him, against all the bottles he's ever emptied
and against the mud stuck to his feet, kicks
    and kicks through the clutches of soaked jeans
        that cling to his legs, kicks himself
for still living in Smyrna, for still
    living, pulls through the underwater rumble
        of tugs pushing barges upriver, swims hard
till his chest burns and head throbs and he finally breaks
    the surface and sucks in great gulps of air.
        The water is cold and black. He drifts on his back
past a barge heaped high with scrap metal. He was wrong.
    The river is an artery, he thinks, he a blood cell
        floating—alone—amid all the plaque.

January 2009: For Anthony

thirty weeks

As if to herald your coming, miracles
on the nightly news. A woman gives birth
to octuplets: in California, her nursery
holds eight wooden cribs
for the preschool class
conceived in a lab and implanted
aboard the minuscule school bus
of her uterus.

A plane sets down on the Hudson.
Passengers of US Airways 1549
stand on the aircraft's wings,
and though I know it's all physics
and well-trained flight attendants,
they walk on water.

In the frigid air of the Capitol steps,
a man born at the crossroads
of Kansas and Kenya
takes the oath of office. A historic first.
Next day, a historic second—
the man sworn in all over again
since the black robe bungled his lines.

These, Anthony, are the everyday
wonders that pass for news, and history,
that, inching toward the vanishing point
of time, all become trivia
or less, molecules, hydrogen and oxygen
rushing downriver to join the ocean.

If I have wisdom,
it's this: question miracles
and believe,
for you are one
and you aren't.

Pfc. Mason Buxton, Home from Work

After pecks on the cheek, his wife
　　　　and baby retreat to the farthest room
　　　　　　　from him, the tiny guest bedroom
　　　　where he sometimes sleeps to escape
the night crying, the waking to breastfeed,

the pitiful whimpers drifting from the crib.
　　　　Even the dog keeps her distance
　　　　　　　and a concerned silence, gnawing
　　　　a ragged shoe with the laces removed.
Into a chair he melts for half an hour,

rocking in silence. When the sun sets
　　　　behind a neighbor's house, he rises,
　　　　　　　plods down the hall, asks to hold the baby,
　　　　and when she lets out a hearty cry
the whole house exhales for the first time.

Cooking Fried Rice

My wife's white-socked feet
polish the gray vinyl tile of our kitchen.
She spins from fridge to stove
while I stand at the cutting board,
cilantro on the altar, a sacrifice
to the tiny tongue-throned gods
of our taste buds
who, later, will convene in a kiss
like the pantheon on Olympus
or fallen angels in the lake of fire.

Maybe it's the garlic,
the pungent onion, the ginger singed
in hot oil spreading itself
over the base of the wok,
or else the cilantro's scent
wafting its message, *I am green,*
I am the essence of freshness,
like wisps of smoke from a censer,
this choir of fragrance chanting praise
in harmony amid the stained-glass hues
of carrot, tomato, spinach,
whatever progeny of earth and seed
she's found in the crisper,
while rice simmers on the back burner,
white bubbles pressed together,
rising, lifting the glass lid till it rattles

and, senses buzzing, she breaks
into motion, some jaunty bounce,
knees bent, arms raised, the dance
of a child who has not learned
to fear, of a priestess
enthralled, of a woman in love.
She stays the knife beneath my hand,
pulls me into her movements,
and—two bubbles conjoined—
our bodies make a single swaying temple.

The pecan pie takes a week to eat

alone. I'm reheating it—again—
so I call over the hard-jawed
mechanic from the shop next door.
Two weeks I've watched him tinker
well past quitting time
when his partner leaves
and he untucks his shirt,
flips the sign in the window
to CLOSED. Out back, his house
sags between pines, empty

as a widow's bed. He's young,
my second daughter's age,
I'd guess, says, *Yes ma'am,*
when I ask if business is good,
Something's always breaking down
in this town. Quietly, he fidgets
at the table's head, stroking
a patchscratch beard with nails
trimmed to the quick. His form
fills the room like a stud
in a filly's stable. He eats
faster than I want him to,
so I pour more coffee. He takes it
black. His bloodshot eyes make me think
of a tin pie plate scored
with the slicing of a hundred pies.
I cover what remains with foil,
send him *Thank you ma'am*-ing home
with pie and plate and knife.

I brush crumbs into my hand.
Shake them into the sink. I settle in
for the two or three patient days
till he'll tap lightly at my door
—my truest friend—
a big strong man with a knife
and an empty tin.

Deer

thirty-six weeks

At first each car-struck carcass seems
unique. But soon they are the same:
tan hides all hanging limply on
their racks of broken ribs, coarse tufts
of fur atremble in the wind,
what's left of their long and elegant necks
twisted or bent at sharp angles.
As we rave on with Buddy Holly
along I-10 on our route home
from San Antonio, your mother and I
count seventy-three before scrub oak,
mesquite, and gentle hills flatten
into newly furrowed cotton fields.
My left hand on the wheel, I reach
my right to her tautly domed abdomen.
Your knee bucks wildly beneath her skin.
Already I wonder who will be first
to die. When the music stops, we drift
into silent thought, and I am wrapped
in a tawny pelt, like an old Comanche
stalking prey—my spine the deer's,
its ribcage hugging mine. Collapsed
in dry bunch grass, I see the vultures
have gathered. But my breath revives
the deer, and they scatter. I rise. I bolt
from the roadside, leap a barbed-wire fence.

Esther Dreams of Floyd for the Third Straight Night

So many reasons this is wrong—
he's much too young for me,
I'm six short months a widow . . .
But he comes to me again,
this time in a lowland forest
where wildflowers open to drink
the dew, scents of cypress and pine
rise, and gray limbs sift the lazy sunlight
playing across my paisley bed.
On a stump: a stoneware carafe,
a green bar of Lava,
Granny's ceramic basin
—bone-dry on the dresser for decades,
it held Bill's wallet and smokes.
Overhead, wind rustles Spanish moss
like the hair of some woodland fairy.

I take Floyd by the bicep,
lead him to the stump.
I pick up the carafe and pour
until the basin is full, take the soap
and wash away the engine grease
from Floyd's thick, heavy hands,
which then leave their wet prints
on my hip and back. I slip
each blue button of his shirt
through its hole, a row of keys
unlocking a door to the secret
garden in a book I once read
to my girls. His kisses
taste of pecan pie

as we fumble toward the bed.
He likes the softness of my body.
Our clothes have disappeared,
I'm locked in the curves of his arms
when I hear the crunch of leaves underfoot

and I push Floyd away, fold into myself
like a morning glory at midnight.
I'm curled tight beneath the sheet,
in tears, when at the foot of the bed,
there's Bill, a Winston slung between his lips,
the fishing line strung from his cane pole
vanishing into Granny's basin
as if it held an entire lake. The cane tip
bobbles and dips, and Bill pulls out a fish,
a good-sized bluegill. Carefully,
he wraps his hand around the fish's fins,
then pulls from its stuttering mouth
a silver coin. He drops the fish into the carafe,
then flips the coin with his thumb,
snatches it out of the air, grins,
and says, *Go on, Queenie, it's all right by me.*

That's when I wake, alone and small
in our queen-sized bed. I pull
to my face the faded bedspread, inhale
the odor—barely there—of cigarettes.

V

Claudia Blackwood Has Her Doubts

1

It's unbecoming of a preacher's wife,
these thoughts that worm their way into my brain
like hairline cracks in ancient porcelain,
then cobweb into chinks. Or weeds run rife
in a garden—nutsedge, crabgrass, purple loosestrife,
a climbing blanket of kudzu laying claim
to the pergola where roses once were trained—
those seeds always the first to spring to life.

But isn't everyone entitled to
their doubts? What farmer hasn't lost some sleep
reckoning if his crop will make or not?
Though he, at least, don't need to hide his thoughts
from pals down at the donut shop. I keep
tight-lipped, sit pretty in the second pew.

2

Tight-lipped, I sit pretty in the second pew
beside our angel Mary Ruth, dispense
Crayolas. Sometimes I wish she'd scribble through
those thick black lines. They hold her like a fence.

Meanwhile her daddy, who even I call Pastor,
is up there preaching the New Testament
in tones first soft and slow, then louder, faster:
Heaven or Hell, the choice is yours! Repent!

I nod at the right times, and shout, *Amen!*
a time or two. But maybe this is just
a hoax, a sacred land-sale scam, and when
we die we'll each last one of us go bust . . .

The others all sit mesmerized, starstruck.
I go set out the chicken for the potluck.

3

I go set out the chicken for the potluck,
sweeten up the tea. They'll be a while
yet—the pianist's first chords just struck,
and Pastor will wait till someone walks the aisle.

But each time someone has, what has it meant?
Was it their choice? A still-small-voiced suggestion?
Is Pastor truly the Lord's instrument?
Or maybe that "gut feeling" is indigestion.

Or else it's all mapped out right from the start,
you're in or you ain't, and there's nothing you can do
to change one whit, like if you're tall or short
or black or white or Eskimo or Jew.

If that's the way it is, then what's the use
of walking down the aisle? It's all a ruse.

4

Walking down the aisle's just a ruse
if God welcomes His elect to Paradise,
then squishes lesser ones of us like lice
in a beggar's beard (picked wriggling from the face
and held by holy finger and thumb, we brace
ourselves against the eternal pinch, the price
for our unchosenness). Naughty or nice,
He done fixed your final resting place.

Then what of the eleventh-hour conversion?
Repentant death-row killers, thief on the cross—
would God damn me and choose a common crook?
No lover prefers the harlot to the virgin.
No jeweler refuses gold to work with dross.
Have I not always done things by the book?

5

Have I? Not always—I done things. Good Book
says we all have sinned. (The napkins, sporks,
the knives: all set.) But I do good; I took
poor Esther dinner, bless her heart. "Not works
but grace," though, Pastor says, "lest men should boast."
That's truth, and yet I smell a paradox—
"by grace through faith," but isn't faith supposed
to bring good works? One's grain, the other an ox
that pulls the plow, breaking hard-baked earth
into rows of loamy soil, dark and rich
for planting, and when it's done its day of work,
it feeds on last year's harvest. But which is which?

Sounds like they're done—that voice I hear is Pastor
with Mary Ruth. Now who is that with Esther?

6

Who *is* that long-haired gentleman with Esther?
They put him first in line—he must have walked.
Well, glory be! A wing, or thigh, or breast, or
drumstick? My, how quietly he talks.

I walked when I was only nine, a girl
in a floral knee-length sack and an Easter bonnet.
I got baptized, and all was right with the world.
Now I've had twenty years to ponder on it,
and faith seems harder the longer I believe.

When Jacob pinned that angel to the ground,
the dislocated hip that he received
came with a blessing. Sometimes I feel that way—
that someday God is bound to come around
if I keep holding on, come what may.

7

So I keep on holding on, come what may.
But take a look around Fellowship Hall:
tables full of greasy-fingered faithful.
Do they swallow what is fed them, bones and all?
Judging from their plates, don't look that way.
Then why do we all act like doubt is shameful?

There's . . . Floyd, he said, is his name. Pastor's got him
cornered, poor thing. Won't let him eat in peace.
I've seen his type. He finally hits rock bottom.
"Gets saved." Then goes back to his vice.

And Mary Ruth just clings to her daddy's waist.
Someday she'll walk. Someday she'll have my life.
Do something, Claudia. Grab Esther's sleeve. Say:
It's unbecoming of a preacher's wife . . .

Moonrise

An impossible orange moon
slimmed with two days' waning
creeps over the wan horizon

as I drive the five hours home
from the Albuquerque airport
this Easter night, my wife

asleep on the back seat.
For a minute the disk appears
to rest at the end of the road,

a final destination,
and I half   expect a sign:
MOON 36 MILES.

Heavy and stolid, it lolls
like the flat, round stone
that sealed the tomb of Christ

in the picture Bible I had
as a child and read religiously,
as others read comic books,

and yet it seems weightless as space,
as air, this moon, this lunar
optical illusion

floating into the sky
as Earth turns in her sleep.
The hours pass, and it grows

smaller but brighter, not orange
but now the color of eggs
before my two nephews dyed them

last night. Eleven o'clock,
too late now to call my mother,
assure her that we're safe,

though she will lie awake,
draped in the haze of her fears
of missed flights, delays, or worse.

I still remember how
she woke us every Easter:
He is risen! To which we said

He is risen indeed! and we dashed
past her to the den,
knowing the resurrection

also meant chocolate bunnies
in the pastel plastic baskets
Dad stored in the attic.

Where are those photos she took
each year of my clip-on tie,
my sister's ridiculous hat?

Or of the year at my aunt's,
a family of live rabbits
hopping from a hole in their yard?

Those pictures—stuffed in a shoebox?
Or lost, thrown out by mistake,
discarded during a move?

Maybe sometimes we get it
right by accident,
trade mementos for memories

and mystery. By midnight,
the moon overhead is tiny,
a flat, white wafer,

or the distant, secret home
of a comic book hero
boys conjure in their dreams.

Or a cratered satellite
held in orbit by its nearness
to our planet's greater mass.

But watching it now I recall
from Eucharist this morning
the dry, plain starch of the Host—

like flour and cardboard mixed
with the salt from a drop of sweat—
as it broke apart in my mouth.

And I see it whole again,
shining like an oiled wound
in the night sky's side.

Cut

forty weeks, three days

Twined deep inside,
a ladder of three
billion rungs
twisting upward
then doubling back
in an endless tangle,
ropes of code
binding us to you,
you to us:
we form a nucleus.

                    •

Our Heavenly Father,
I learned to pray,
and I found the title comforting,
for a father was something
I was not: strong, wise,
dependable as a sandwich
at lunchtime. But now,
on the verge, how
am I to pray?

                    •

A table saw hunches
on my family's back porch,
its gleaming teeth
a diamond-dusted arc
cresting the black cast metal
right at eye level. Our lawn:

a lumberyard. My father
is building cabinets to hang
in our kitchen. I am five.
Dad hollers to stand back,
flips the switch. He rips
a white sheet of maple plywood
into perfect rectangles, the blade
screaming with every cut. Fingers
rammed in my ears, I watch
the sawdust shower my sneakers,
inhale the taste of a tree.

•

Wander museums of sacred art
with an eye to those portraits,
cobalt and gold,
of the Holy Family: Joseph
and doe-eyed Mary peering down
at the infant, who gazes out at you
with eerie serenity.
See how they plot three points,
or form three lines,
geometrically composed.
Then go look for Christ on the cross,
his haloed mother weeping at his feet.
Observe her grief in every Pietà,
her flaming heart pierced through
with swords, ringed with thorny roses.
Now return to those Nativities.
Notice the shape of those triangles:
scalene. Search Joseph's eyes
for the telltale signs of a man
who knows he's in too deep.
See him already fading
into the field of blue?

•

A prayer from the Psalms:
Do not hold against us the sins of the fathers;
may your mercy come quickly to meet us,
for we are in desperate need.
Learn it well.

•

Dad hauls the boards inside and I
return to my own construction:
I am hammering nails
into a scrap of two-by-four,
making beds for G.I. Joes.
I'll present it to him when I'm done,
an offering resembling nothing
more than a bed of half-bent nails.
But now I set the hammer down, turn
to face the monster looming over me.
I trace the C-R-A-F-T-S-M-A-N,
touch the parts I have not learned
to name: rip fence, miter gauge.
The shark-toothed pinwheel
peeping from the tabletop
begs to be touched. I rise
on the tips of my toes, stretch,
and my finger sings a red song.

•

You are blood of my blood.
Wharton's jelly protects
the vein and two arteries
that link you to your mother
as you and I can never be linked.

A cord of three strands,
Ecclesiastes says, is not easily broken.
Why fear the rope unraveling? Why
worry the fibers will fray?

•

The poem I wish I could write
says I will never give you a stone
when you ask for bread, never
a snake when you ask for fish.
May your teeth be as diamonds,
your tongue as a charmer's flute.

•

I am twelve and my brother four
and I do not want to "bunk together."
But he's outgrown his toddler bed,
so Dad is back at the saw.
I'm working on my jump shot in the driveway,
but he calls for me every five minutes
to hold in place the measuring tape,
pencil a line to mark the cut,
help with this and that,
the saw shrieking noisy as hell
and filming my kicks with dust,
and he doesn't really need my help,
but, *Let me show you how,* he says,
But I'm practicing my follow-through, I say,
But this is your bed I'm making, he says,
and I say, *Then I'll sleep on the goddam floor.*
At least go stack those two-by-fours, he says,
and he flips the switch. He cuts a clean edge,
careful to follow through, guiding
the fresh-cut boards clear of the blade.

LOVE'S LABORS

•

Tradition holds that Joseph died
sometime during the years of Gospel silence
between pre-teen Jesus wowing the priests
and the thirty-year-old Christ
turning water into wine.
But he must have lived long enough
to train his Lord in the family trade,
put calluses on those holy hands
by giving them hammer and plane and saw.
He knew that well-built things outlast us,
and so he taught the boy to build.

•

In the softened, artificial light of Labor
and Delivery, now the middle of the night,
for hours the nurse has turned your mother
thus and thus, hoping you'll move
into the proper pose, head down, face back,
but even in utero you are strong-willed.
You're facing one side, your shoulders
squared against your mother's hips.
When it's time to push, the doc
calls for the vacuum extractor
discreetly, so as not to cause alarm,
and someone turns on brighter lights.
The device looks something like a plunger
in miniature, which the doc affixes to your head
still deep inside your mother's body,
and when, teeth gritted, groaning, she strains
with all her strength, he pulls
and twists the thing with all of his.
But you'll have none of it.
You turn the other way, face front.

Between each push I deliver chips of ice
into her mouth. While she crunches a spoonful
he whispers for a nurse to bring the scissors.
Anesthetized, your mother can't feel
when he opens up her flesh,
but still he casts apologetic eyes.
A couple pushes more and your head is out.
Your mother cannot see you yet,
but you and I are face to face. You do not cry
at first. I cannot breathe: there's something wrong.
You blink at me as if to say, *Well,*
and what do you propose to do about it?

•

At twenty-two I come around,
begin to see my father as more of me
than I can safely excise,
a gnarled knot in a block of wood
that will splinter the whole into shards
if a cut is made too close.
But I also know, at last,
the knot gives the wood its grain,
find no reason for wanting it gone.
Instead I want the snug joint
of friendship, the perfectly planed edge
of wisdom sanded smooth
by the passing of years
like coarse-grit paper followed by fine-.
And so it's back to the table saw,
no longer the hulk I once knew,
its legs showing spots of rust
though the table is freshly oiled,
standing now in its own cool quarters,
a workshop on one end of the garage
at the house my parents built.

LOVE'S LABORS

•

Would I remove from your lips,
if I could, the cup of suffering?
Would you drink it even if I tried?
Our Father who art in Heaven,
call this an act of faith—
bringing new life into the crucified world,
world of lashes and thorns,
of *Father, why*
have you forsaken me? and *Father,*
into your hands I commit my spirit.
Dear Saint Joseph, Mother Mary,
pray for us,
for we are in desperate need.

•

Dad helps me select the boards of golden oak
we'll use to make the small bookcase I've sketched
on paper lined with small, blue squares.
He coaches me as I guide the wood
toward the spinning, whirring blade.
It sings out and sawdust flies
like wind-stirred snow. Invisible particles
collect in our nostrils, stick to our tongues,
and the garage smells like a forest
or a homesite, or both.
For weeks my nights are lit
by the workshop's fluorescent tubes
and call forth the mechanical tunes
of routers and sanders and drills and saws,
our voices filling the interstitial calm.
With clumsy hands I gouge the panels
and nick the beveled edge,
and somehow the thing's not square;

but when, with a piece of tack cloth,
I wipe away the final motes of dust
from each stained and varnished shelf,
it's more than my books they hold.

•

I have only just made peace
with having a father,
and here you are to make me one.
Blood and vernix and milia
cover you—flat-nosed, puffy-eyed,
cone-headed, flushed and wailing
and wet in the nurse's hands.
Your mother waits for you.
In my left hand a clamp,
scissors in my right. The blades
bite down.

ACKNOWLEDGMENTS

I am grateful to the editors of the journals and anthologies in which these poems first appeared, sometimes in earlier versions:

America: "Ode to the Heart" (awarded the 2009 Foley Poetry Prize)

Best New Poets 2010 (Samovar Press)*:* "Esther Green Moves Out of the Sunset Acres Mobile Home Community"

Birmingham Poetry Review: "Saint Gerard"

Cave Wall: "Agriculture," "The pecan pie takes a week to eat"

Cresset: "Desire," "January 2009: For Anthony"

Grist: "Pfc. Mason Buxton Embraces the Suck"

The Gulf Stream: Poems of the Gulf Coast (Snake Nation Press)*:* "Esther Dreams of Floyd for the Third Straight Night," "Smyrna"

Hopkins Review: "Inheritance"

Louisiana Literature: "Claudia Blackwood Has Her Doubts"

Luna Luna: "Internal Combustion"

Mamas and Papas: On the Sublime and Heartbreaking Art of Parenting (City Works Press): "Strawberries"

Measure: "How Floyd Fontenot Lost His Father"

New Delta Review: "Floyd Fontenot's Friday Night," "Needing a Day Away from Smyrna, Floyd Fontenot Winds Up in Baton Rouge, on the East Bank of the Mississippi"

New Texas: "Turbulence"

Oklahoma Review: "Ash Wednesday," "Esther Green Plans a Funeral," "Floyd and Patti," "Floyd Fontenot, Free Bird," "New Hope Baptist Church"

PANK: "Smyrna"

REAL: "Deer"

Relief: "Christmas Day," "Fête," "First Ultrasound"

Southern Review: "Pfc. Mason Buxton, Home from Work"

Subtropics: "Pfc. Mason Buxton Wets a Hook"

Tar River Poetry: "Cooking Fried Rice"

Windhover: "Ava," "Epithalamion"

Fellowships from Texas Tech University and the U.S. Fulbright Program provided financial support during the writing of many of these poems. I am also grateful for the friendship, encouragement, and constructive criticism of many fellow writers and mentors whose wisdom and goodwill aided me along the way: Aaron Alford, Lauri Anderson Alford, Curtis Bauer, Vincent Cellucci, Eric Elliott, Nimi Finnigan, Jonathan Bohr Heinen, Adam Houle, Carrie Jerrell, Benjamin Lowenkron, Jessicca Daigle Martin, Laura Mullen, Jill Patterson, Richard Pierce, Ruben Quesada, Randolph Thomas, John Poch, Jacqueline Kolosov, and especially William Wenthe. Thanks to Mom, Dad, Andrea, Jason, and Mark for years of love and support and to Anthony and Molly for bringing me such joy. To my wife, Amanda, more thanks are due than I can express. You keep me going.

NOTES

I am indebted to a March 8, 2007, NPR story on Austin Bay's book *"Embrace the Suck": A Pocket Guide to Milspeak* for much of the language in "Pfc. Mason Buxton Embraces the Suck."

When writing the several poems that use automotive and mechanical language, imagery, and themes, I referred repeatedly to two books. John L. Lumley's *Engines: An Introduction* was instrumental in explaining to this mechanical novice how engines work; Edwin Black's *Internal Combustion* gave a thought-provoking analysis of the social effects of engines and automobiles on American culture, history, and politics.

CAVANKERRY'S MISSION

CavanKerry Press is committed to expanding the reach of poetry
to a general readership by publishing poets whose works explore
the emotional and psychological landscapes of everyday life.

OTHER BOOKS IN THE EMERGING VOICES SERIES

The text of this book was typeset in Adobe Garamond, a variant of the Garamond font, which has a very long history. The font is named for its designer, Claude Garamond, who based his design on type originally cut by Francesco Griffo in 1455.